The
Next Great
Reformation

96
New Theses

for reclaiming Jesus' everlasting kingdom

JOHN NOĒ, Ph.D.

The Next Great Reformation

By John Noē, Ph.D.

Unless otherwise noted, all Scripture quotations are from the Holy Bible, *New International Version* © 1973, 1978, 1984 International Bible Society. Used by permission of Zondervan Bible Publishers.

Published by:
East2West Press
Publishing arm of the Prophecy Reformation Institute
5236 East 72nd Street
Indianapolis, IN 46250 USA

Cover: Donated by Tom Haulter
ebook conversion and initial marketing : Donated by
Patrick Linsenmeyer at Createbook.org

<u>*Cover picture symbolism*</u>: King Jesus and his queen—the bride, the wife of the Lamb, the overcomers in the Church—i.e., those who are reigning and ruling with Him in his kingdom on this earth, here and now (see Rev. 21:1-10; 1:4-6; 5:9-10; 12:10-11; John 14:12; and more).

ISBN: 978-0-9834303-8-4
Library of Congress Control Number: 2016919301

Kingdom. Eschatology. Bible. Jesus. Old Testament Revelation. New Testament Revelation

Dedication

To Dr. James Earl Massey (see p. 39) who took me under his wing and privately mentored me for two years during the late 1990s. You were the first to suggest the following on the back cover of my book then titled, *Beyond the End Times* (1999):

"Noe's book just could be the spark that ignites
the next reformation of Christianity."

To my 29 cosigners of
"9.5 Theses for the Next Reformation."
Together we posted that document on the "door" of
the 53rd Annual Meeting of the Evangelical Theological Society
held in Colorado Springs, Colorado, November 14-16, 2001.
We earnestly desired to see that reformation launched, then and there.
But we, our dream, and that document were largely ignored.

To my many readers over the years.
You have afforded me the honor and privilege
to serve as a writer and a teacher.
Without you, my efforts would be in vain.

Lastly, to those who will stand on my shoulders
to disseminate, dispute, discuss, debate, and advance these
"96 New Theses" for *The Next Great Reformation*
in the years and generations ahead.

CONTACT US:

Prophecy Reformation Institute
5236 East 72nd Street
Indianapolis, IN 46250
Website: prophecyrefi.org
jnoe@prophecyrefi.org
Ph. # 317-842-3411

Contents

Introduction

'For Such a Time as This' —on the 500th Anniversary?

About every 500 years, a pivotal event and revolutionary upheaval has transpired in Christian history Each set in motion a major turning point and transformation. Each also launched a more vital form and expansion of our faith. This semi-millennial trend or theory is termed "the 500-year cycle." Author and former Publisher's Weekly religion editor Phyllis Tickle claims such an upheaval is happening now. In her book, *The Great Emergence* (2012), she highlights these events in this recurrent pattern:

- 0 – the time of Jesus and Christianity is born out of Judaism.
- 476 – fall of the Roman Empire and start of the monastic movement.
- 1054 – the Great Schism splits the eastern and western churches.
- 1517 – start of the Protestant or Great Reformation.
- 2012 – a "great emergence" is underway.
- 2017 – the 500th Anniversary.

In 2012, Tickle did not specify what this great emergence might be, or involve. But I will. Boldly, prayerfully, and perhaps prophetically, I propose the following initiative and invitation for your consideration, testing, input, and involvement—"for such a time as this" (Esther 4:14b).

As we approach this 500th anniversary, wouldn't it be just like God to choose this time for moving us into The Next Great Reformation? Therein, his Church and all believers would better understand its and their purpose to reign and rule on earth under the lordship of Jesus Christ and for advancing his everlasting and ever-increasing kingdom.

The fact is, the two great works of the Messiah were that of the kingdom and that of salvation.

- That's the order in which Jesus announced them.
- That's the order in which He accomplished them.

Hence, October 31, 2017, marks a seminal moment in church and world history. On this date in 1517 (allegedly), Martin Luther nailed (posted) his "95 Theses" to the door (bulletin board) of his home church in Wittenberg, Germany. But his theses and the subsequent reformation primarily addressed salvation issues (such as indulgences) along with the authority and accessibility of Scripture and the power and authority of the Pope, Roman Catholic Church, and its clergy.

Therefore, I propose that this 500th Anniversary in 2017 be the year for launching The Next Great Reformation of Christianity:

- It should center on the other great work of the Messiah—that of the kingdom, its issues, and grounding it time- and nature-wise.
- Perhaps we call it the "Kingdom Reformation."
- Facts are that the kingdom was the central teaching of Jesus.
- But today the kingdom is no longer the central teaching of most of his Church.
- Instead, Jesus' kingdom is caught up in eschatological mid-air and one of the most misunderstood, misconstrued, marginalized, confused, abstracted, abused, contested, and ignored realities of Christianity.
- And we are reaping mighty consequences.

[Note to reader: the above introductory information will be reincorporated in our next section as theses in the "96 New Theses."]

Reformation Comparative and Historical Parallels

<u>1517</u>	<u>2017</u>
• Catholic clergy massively misleading Christians regarding salvation issues (such as indulgences) along with the authority of the Pope and RCC.	• Church leadership massively misleading Christians regarding kingdom issues, such as its time, nature, and present-day status.
• Martin Luther faces major difficulty breaking through church resistance, getting heard, and considered.	• I, and others, face the same difficulty in churches, with Christian publishers, the media, and in academia.
• On October 31, (allegedly) Luther initiates and ignites his Great Reformation with a bold strategy and step. He nails (posts) his "95 Theses" to the door of his home church in Wittenberg, Germany.	• Today, there is no single "door" on which to nail (post) or one "Wittenberg" from which to dispute these "96 New Theses" for the "Kingdom Reformation." Rather, there are many "doors" and "churches."
• Despite Wittenberg being a small and poor town in central Germany, he attracts key people to join with him. Together, they recover a vital portion of the truth of God's Word, transform Europe, and redirect the course of Christianity. It all played out in the public theater.	• Many of us are also located in small towns. But we, too, can attract key people to join with us to help disseminate and dispute on these "96 New Theses for reclaiming Jesus' everlasting kingdom." Together, we, too, can be the spark that ignites The Next Great Reformation.

<u>**1517**</u>	<u>**2017**</u>
• The church in Wittenberg becomes the launching platform, home base, magnet, and training, equipping, and disputation center for those throughout Germany and beyond. From here this Great Reformation is championed, advocated, and advanced, and Protestantism is birthed.	• Likewise, this Next Great Reformation would benefit from an influential church, churches, and/or major ministry becoming the "Wittenberg"—i.e. the home base and center for launching, disputing, and advancing this "Kingdom Reformation." (To be determined.)
• Luther and others speak out passionately, persuasively, and often on Reformation issues.	• And so must we in making our "96 New Theses" known and to reclaim this central teaching of Jesus.
• The Reformation would not have occurred as it did without published and compelling materials.	• We, too, have a published and compelling body of knowledge to disseminate for wider public impact.
• That Reformation blazed on for more than a hundred years—a pivotal era in human and church history.	• We can only launch it. Then we must pass it on in a well-developed and sustainable manner to others.
• From their perseverance it grew into a mighty worldwide movement.	• But that first Reformation did not go far enough. It stopped short.
• Thus, Luther and his many pioneering partners met their moment of destiny with extraordinary boldness, skill, and resourcefulness.	• Will we? Will you? Most certainly, **"Here I stand. I cannot do otherwise."** But this endeavor cannot be the work of a single person.

<u>Indeed, a reformation is greater than a revival or an awakening</u>. But revivals and awakenings can be by-products thereof. Another by-product could be the unifying of other diverse theological leanings among evangelicals, all of which would change the face of Christianity for the better—how it is preached, practiced, and perceived.

Also, please be advised—this reformational vision is not solely mine.

Supportive Insights and Quotations

Many today feel a crying need for something bold, different, and dynamic to break through the confusion, complacency, divisiveness, and brokenness in our world and churches. What's needed is something significant and inspiring to rally behind and around. I believe that "something" is to reclaim the central teaching of Jesus and advance his fully established, everlasting, and ever-increasing kingdom throughout the church and our world. Might this just be God's call of destiny?

What have we to lose? What have we to gain? Perhaps we, too, have come into the world "for such a time as this." Martin Luther did. And other pioneering partners joined with him in their day and time. Why not us? Isn't it time we reclaim the other great work of the Messiah?

In his insightful book, *Brand Luther*,[1] Andrew Pettegree aptly summarizes the involvement dynamics that were necessary to launch, advance, and sustain the previous Reformation **"over the heads of his clerical brethren to a wider popular audience" (p. 216):**

> However eagerly Luther's books were circulated and read, this in itself would not have been sufficient. It required the emergence of leaders, of trusted and respected local figures, prepared to commit themselves openly to the cause. This required great courage. . . . Many put their lives and certainly their livelihoods, at risk by speaking up for Luther and the Gospel teaching . . . . These, in many ways, were the boldest of the Reformation's pioneers . . . moved solely by their sense of the rightness of the new evangelical

---

[1] Andrew Pettegree, *Brand Luther* (New York, NY.: Penguin Press, 2015).

doctrines. . . . None of them had any known previous association with Luther; they must have been converted through reading his books. . . . Luther deserved to be heard rather than condemned. . . . It was an extraordinary legacy . . . . (pp. 199, 205, 229, 338).

So it happened in this manner. Likewise, I maintain that these same involvement dynamics are just as necessary today, if not more so, to bring about this Next Great Reformation, its reclaiming of Jesus' kingdom, and a re-configuration of Christianity. This reformation will certainly transform more than just the way we do or don't "do church."

Prophetically, Mark Batterson proclaims this same visionary perspective in his book: *Draw the Circle:*[2]

Reformation

At critical junctures in history, God raises up a remnant to reestablish His reign and rule. It's rarely a majority. In fact, it's almost always a small minority. But all it takes is a faithful few to begin a reformation.

It's not a new discovery that sparks it. Reformations are birthed out of rediscovering something ancient, something simple, something true. . . . All it takes is a remnant rising up! . . . It's time to rise up. It's time for reformation. The next great awakening. . . (pp. 189-191).

Although Batterson does not mention what this next great awakening and reformation might be, I do. John Hampton in his new book, *Flatlining,*[3] echoes this same prophetic refrain:

Today, a variety of methods are employed in an attempt to inject some adrenaline into a flagging body: the response within some circles is to preach relentlessly on impending revival . . . . The church at large, however, needs something more akin to a Second Reformation. . . . It would require something of biblical proportions. (p. 317-318).

---

[2] Mark Batterson, *Draw the Circle: The 40 Day Prayer Challenge* (Grand Rapids, MI.: Zondervan, 2012).
[3] John Hampton, *Flatlining* (n.p., 2016).

In 2017, that "Second Reformation" that "something" should become the rediscovery and reclaiming of Christ's fully established, everlasting, and ever-increasing kingdom—the other great work of the Messiah. To do so will require a teaming up of pioneering partners to attract, educate, motivate, and equip others for the glory of God and the mutual benefit of all humankind.

Lastly, I'll offer these quotes from my pastor Dave Rodriguez. He delivered them during his sermon of April 23-24, 2016:

- **"A small group of thoughtful people could change the world. Indeed, it's the only thing that ever has." – Margaret Mead**
- **"The people who are crazy enough to think they can change the world are the ones who do." –** *Unknown*

Becoming a Pioneering Partner

As you are about to see, these "96 New Theses" are concise and to the point. They are also provocative, compelling, and patterned after Luther's "95 Theses." Some may consider them controversial. But they flow systematically following the greater content of the book from which they are largely drawn[4] (see next page).

One advantage of a full-length book, over this shorter booklet, is the amount of supportive and interactive information that can be shared. For this reason, I recommend this source book to your further attention.

Lastly, thank you for considering these "96 New Theses." I hope they encourage you to partner with us in this timely initiative and monumental endeavor. Sincerely, I believe the destiny of America, the world, our children, grandchildren, and future generations, is at stake. Therefore, will you join with us as a pioneering partner to help us get this Next-Great-Reformation message out, heard, and spread in your circles of influence?

---

[4] John Noē, *A Once Mighty Faith: Reclaiming the central teaching of Jesus, reengaging the miraculous* (Indianapolis, IN.: East2West Press, 2016).

What They Are Saying about . . .

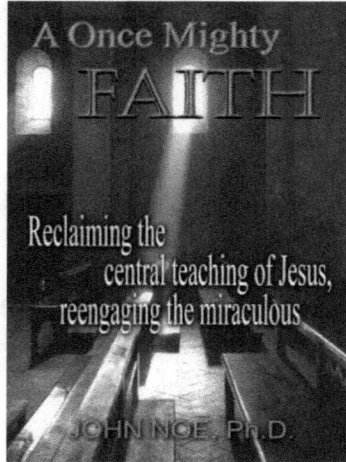

You likely have not heard of John Noē, but once you read this book you will not forget him. John has captured the central teaching of Jesus like no others have. It is provocative, eye-opening, inspiring, and deeply biblical. Even if you don't agree with him at times, you will find yourself motivated to engage yourself and your church in the great world-altering Kingdom of God! Yes, we can change the world in Jesus' name!

(Dave Rodriguez, Senior Pastor, Grace Church, Noblesville, IN)

This book is weighty but well-worth exploring. As an evangelistic communicator, I must continue probing the riches of the biblical message of the Kingdom of God through Jesus Christ. I have been stretched significantly from reading this book, and am still processing it!

John has provided a very unique perspective. I have never heard anyone present these concepts this way, nor connect various items as he does—such as our eschatological views impacting our actions in the Kingdom of God, and many more. This could be John's *magnum opus*.

If John's conclusions are correct and if they were then lived out by Christians, it could literally have significant consequences of epic proportions for the Christian church.

(Mark Slaughter, Evangelist, InterVarsity Christian Fellowship)

For more reviews and to "Look Inside," go to: Amazon.com

96 New Theses

for Reclaiming Jesus' Everlasting Kingdom[5]

Disputation on reductions of the central teaching of Jesus—the kingdom of God—and Jesus as King

(Largely drawn from: *A Once Mighty Faith: Reclaiming the central teaching of Jesus; reengaging the miraculous*, a 2016 book by John Noē)

Out of love for the truth and a desire to elucidate it, John Noē and fellow reformers intend to defend the following statements and to dispute on them. We further desire to see all Christians acknowledge and honor all that God has revealed in his Word. Hence, we submit these "96 New Theses" for your prayerful evaluation and participation with us in calling for this Next Great Reformation. May these theses be the spark that ignites it as Martin Luther's "95 Theses" initiated the former Great Reformation 500 years ago.

---

[5] These "96 New Theses" are patterned after but different from Martin Luther's "95 Theses." They contain one more thesis, not only to differentiate them but also because the effects of this Next Great Reformation, should it occur, could be greater than the effects of the previous Reformation. For instance, this Next Great Reformation will affect the creeds as well as traditional eschatological paradigms—something Luther's "95 Theses" and Reformation never did.

'For Such a Time as This' (Esther 4:14b)

1. The two great works of the Messiah were that of the kingdom and that of salvation.
2. That's the order in which Jesus announced them; that's the order in which He accomplished them.
3. October 31, 2017 marks a seminal moment in church and world history. On this date in 1517 (allegedly), Martin Luther nailed (posted) his "95 Theses" to the door (bulletin board) of his home church in Wittenberg, Germany.
4. But his theses, also known as the "Disputation on the Power and Efficacy of Indulgences," and the subsequent reformation primarily addressed salvation issues along with the authority and accessibility of Scripture and the power and authority of the Pope, Roman Catholic Church, and its clergy.
5. That first Reformation did not go far enough. It stopped short.
6. About every 500 years, a pivotal event and revolutionary upheaval has transpired in Christian history. Each set in motion a major turning point and transformation. Each also launched a more vital form and expansion of our faith. This semi-millennial trend or theory is termed "the 500-year cycle." Author and former Publisher's Weekly religion editor Phyllis Tickle claims such an upheaval is happening now. In her book, *The Great Emergence* (2012), she highlights these events:

   - 0 – [4 B.C. – A.D. 70] – the time of Jesus and Christianity is born out of Judaism.
   - 476 – fall of the Roman Empire and start of the monastic movement.
   - 1054 – the Great Schism splits the eastern and western churches.
   - 1517 – start of the Protestant or Great Reformation.
   - 2012 – a "great emergence" is underway.
   - 2017 – the 500th Anniversary.

7. In 2012, Tickle did not specify what this great emergence might be, or involve. But I will.

8. As we approach this 500th anniversary, wouldn't it be just like God to choose this time in history for moving us into the Next Great Reformation? Therein his Church and all believers would better understand its and their purpose to reign and rule on earth under the lordship of Jesus Christ and to advance his kingdom.

9. Therefore, I propose that this 500th Anniversary in 2017 be the year for launching this Next Great Reformation of Christianity.

10. It should center on the other great work of the Messiah—that of the kingdom, its issues, and its grounding time- and nature-wise. Perhaps, we call it the "Kingdom Reformation."

11. Indeed, we "have come to the kingdom for such a time as this" (Esther 4:14b, KJV).

The Problems

12. Arguably, the kingdom is the most important and all-encompassing concept of Scripture. So much is contained within it. It was also the central teaching of Jesus. But today the kingdom is no longer the central teaching of most of his Church.

13. Instead, Jesus' kingdom is caught up in eschatological mid-air and one of the most misunderstood, misconstrued, marginalized, confused, abstracted, abused, contested, and ignored realities of Christianity.

14. We are reaping mighty consequences for our kingdom reductions, deficiencies, and confusions—in America and throughout the world.

15. Christianity is accused of having been "tamed." Consequently, non-Christians are being told that they have nothing to fear from Christians.

16. The Gospel has been reduced to only encompassing salvation—i.e., forgiveness of sins, avoiding hell, and going to heaven.

17. But for the first three years of Jesus' three-and-a-half-year earthly ministry his gospel was that of the kingdom.

18. Unfortunately, nowhere did Jesus or any biblical writer define what the kingdom was.

19. So today, the kingdom is a conundrum—a maze of conflict and confusion—that has produced a blinded, weakened, compromised, and marginalized Church.
20. Eschatological divisions drive this conundrum.
21. Dispensational Premillennialists (the most popular view) insist that the kingdom Jesus was presenting is not here anymore. It's been postponed and withdrawn by God. But someday soon Jesus will return and set his kingdom up in a rebuilt temple in Jerusalem for a literal 1,000 years.
22. Amillennialists (the second most popular view) disagree. The kingdom is here but only "in some sense," as a foretaste in eschatological tension between the "already" and "not yet" of partial fulfillment and partial establishment.
23. Postmillennialists (the third most popular view, formerly the most popular view) claim the kingdom is mostly here and will continue to grow, fill, and subdue the earth. But much more is yet to be fulfilled and established when Jesus physically returns.
24. Cessationist Preterists (the least-known view) maintain that the kingdom is here but major components (the supernatural gifts of the Holy Spirit—the charismata) were repossessed by God after the destruction of Jerusalem and the Temple circa A.D. 70. Not all preterists adhere to this cessation view.
25. Additionally, there are these four, popular but unscriptural "kingdom-killer" notions:
26. #1 – Jesus is not yet King.
27. #2 – The kingdom belongs to Israel.
28. #3 – The kingdom won't arrive again until Christ's future 1,000-year reign (Rev. 20:1-10).
29. #4 – The kingdom and the Church are synonymous.
30. Charismatic and Pentecostal leaders admit they are not seeing or experiencing the caliber (quality and quantity) of signs, wonders, miracles, and gifts of the Holy Spirit in their gatherings or ministries as are depicted as normative Christianity in the four gospels and the Book of Acts.
31. But notably, these miraculous manifestations were intrinsic elements of the kingdom Jesus was presenting.

32. Their two main purposes were to signify and demonstrate the arrival of the long-promised kingdom and to authenticate the message (not the messenger) being presented.
33. Today, many of our messages are in open conflict with and contradiction of the messages God was authenticating back then and there, especially in these three areas:
34. #1 – Much of the church presents and practices a different philosophy of ministry—sans the miraculous, doctrinally or functionally.
35. #2 – We present a different gospel—gospel reductionism—removing the kingdom while retaining salvation.
36. #3 – Likewise, we present our different, 19-centuries-delayed-and-counting, eschatological expectations. This conflicts with 1st-century expectations. Their Holy Spirit-led expectations (see John 16:13) were that everything Jesus said was going to happen would happen within their lifetimes.
37. This latter divergence has produced "The Great End-Time Fiasco:" things that were supposed to happen didn't happen as New Testament expectations proved false and forced the Church to invent "delay theory" in direct contradiction of Scripture.
38. Assuredly, big problems call for a big solution.

The Opportunity

39. My Working Great Hypothesis:

   To the degree we modern-day Christians get our faith straightened out so that it harmonizes with the faith depicted in the four gospels and the Book of Acts—the faith God authenticated with signs, wonders, miracles, and gifts of the Holy Spirit following—we may again move the hand of God and begin witnessing the return of these miraculous manifestations at a level approaching 1st-century caliber. Indeed, I believe God is prepared and desires to revive his mighty authenticating powers and blessings to the degree we so move in this direction. Anything less is less.

40. A Mighty Corrective:

> *Our philosophy of ministry must match the 1st-century Church's philosophy of ministry; our gospel message must match their gospel message; our eschatological message must also conform to and confirm that the Holy Spirit-guided imminency expectations of the New Testament writers and the early Church were the correct ones. Anything less is less.*

41. That means: #1 – Returning to the philosophy of ministry Jesus and his disciples taught, practiced, and modeled.
42. #2 – Recovering the full gospel message to encompass the good news of both the kingdom and salvation.
43. #3 – Conforming to and confirming that the 1st-century eschatological expectations were the correct ones, as they pinpointed the imminent fulfillment and establishment of "all things" in their lifetime.

The Solution

44. Grounding the everlasting kingdom—time- and nature-wise.
45. The biblical reality is, as long as there has been a King, there has been a kingdom. God is king and his kingdom (will, reign, and rule) is eternal.
46. But God revealed that there was an appointed time for the arrival of the final form of the everlasting kingdom of God, predicted and anticipated throughout most of the Bible.
47. It would be an eschatological reality brought to earth by the Messiah.
48. According to the prophet Daniel, this everlasting kingdom would arrive in human history "in the days of those kings" (Dan. 2:44).
49. Those four world empires Daniel prophesied thereof were: (Babylon (606 – 538 B.C.), Medo-Persia (538 – 331 B.C.), Greece (331 – 168 B.C.), and the old Roman Empire (168 B.C. – 476 A.D.), respectively.

50. This is why, at the start of his earthly ministry, "Jesus went into Galilee proclaiming the good news of God. The time is fulfilled . . . the kingdom of God is at hand . . . ." (Mark 1:15 KJV).

51. Thus, everything Daniel had prophesied happened in that 1st century A.D. exactly *as* and *when* it was supposed to happen, and precisely *as* and *when* expected (John 16:13). This brings us to four key questions.

52. Question #1 – How many coming kingdoms of God (or forms thereof) were prophesied by Daniel here? THE CORRECT ANSWER IS, "one."

> But dispensational premillennialists' answer is "four." – 1) Jesus' 1st-century kingdom, 2) the withdrawn or present mystery kingdom, 3) the millennial kingdom, 4) the eternal kingdom (when God's will, reign, and rule will be superimposed on all humanity beyond the realm of history—whatever that means). Note: the latter three kingdoms are different-natured from the first.

> Amillennialists' answer is "two." – 1) the present kingdom Jesus brought, which is a foretaste, 2) the eternal-state kingdom in its fullness. Note: the latter kingdom is different-natured from the first.

> Postmillennialists' answer is "two or three." – 1) the present kingdom Jesus brought, 2) a future golden age, 3) the eternal-state kingdom. Note: the latter two kingdoms are different-natured from the first.

> Cessationist Preterists' answer is "two." – 1) the pre-A.D. 70 version of the kingdom brought by Jesus, 2) the post-A.D. 70 spiritual version with major intrinsic elements removed (depending upon whose version one reads, this can include the charismatic gifts, all ministries of the Holy Spirit, the miraculous, even angels). However, not all preterists subscribe to a cessation theology. Note: the latter kingdom is different-natured from the first.

But once again, according to Daniel, there is no other, further, or final manifestation of the kingdom still to come beyond that which Jesus was presenting during his earthly ministry.

53. Question #2 – When would this kingdom be set up? THE CORRECT ANSWER IS, "In the days of those kings." The days of those kings ended in A.D. 476 when the Roman Empire was toppled by Germanic tribes!

54. Question #3 – What do the words "set up" really mean? THE CORRECT ANSWER IS "Established." It was fully established back then, not partially, and was never to be postponed and withdrawn later on.

55. Question #4 – How long would it last? THE CORRECT ANSWER IS, "Forever."

56. Neither dispensational premillennialism's mystery kingdom nor its millennial kingdom in a so-called "revived Roman Empire," "endure[s] forever."

57. Likewise, amillennialism's current kingdom, which was only inaugurated "in the days of those kings," does not "endure forever."

58. Neither does postmillennialism's current kingdom, which was inaugurated "in the days of those kings," nor does its anticipated golden age millennial kingdom "endure forever."

59. None of these futurist views believe the kingdom has come in its fullness. Rather, the dispensationalists, amillennialists, and postmillennialists all variously subscribe to a truncated futuristic time and view.

60. Most distinctly, the everlasting form of the kingdom of God did not arrive, in human and redemptive history, partially established or only initiated, inaugurated, in-breaking, or as a foretaste, already/not yet, "in some sense." Nor was it something to be built or to be established. Nor is it still moving toward a future consummation or completion, as so many have erroneously written and believe. Nor is another kingdom or future upgrade ever mentioned in Scripture. Biblically, the nature of the arrival of the everlasting kingdom does not fit any of these frequently used expressions or descriptions. They are simply products of long-standing traditions of men and erroneous teachings that have plagued the history of Christianity long enough. So why

isn't any of this in-breaking type language used in the Bible? The answer is, for one simple reason:

61. The final form of the everlasting and eschatological kingdom of God arrived *fully established*. Its arrival, however, contrasts with the in-breaking nature for the establishment of salvation—the other great work of the Messiah. Salvation arrived through a series of successive eschatological events, namely, Jesus' birth, earthly ministry, death, burial, resurrection, ascension, Pentecost, the filling up the measure of sin of the Jews, the gospel of the kingdom being preached in all the world, and the destruction and desolation of the Old Covenant, animal-sacrifice, type-and-shadow system.

62. The everlasting form of the kingdom of God, however, arrived *fully established* in the form of a fetus that grew into a babe—"For unto us a child is born" (Isa. 9:6a).

63. Contained within and throughout Jesus' physical body and being was the full incarnation of God's everlasting kingdom—i.e., his will, reign, and rule. Paul confirms this *fully established* arrival, thusly: "For God was pleased to have all fullness dwell in him" (Col. 1:19). "For in Christ all the fullness of the Deity lives in bodily form . . . who is the head over every power and authority" (Col. 2:9-10; also see John 1:14). Therefore, Jesus Christ did not come into this world to *begin* establishing his kingdom, as some assume. The kingdom came with Him, bodily and *fully established*, along with his Kingship. Thus, the Magi aptly and correctly asked, "Where is the one who has been born king of the Jews?" (Matt. 2:2).

64. From that time on and forever, the kingdom would only increase. "Of the increase of his government and peace there will be no end." (Isa. 9:6-7). And so it has been; so it is; so it will be forever.

The Kingdom's Unending Increase

65. With the birth of Jesus "in the days of those kings," the stage is set. The players and pieces are all in place for the kingdom to begin increasing.

66. The baby grows up and at age 12 speaks out in the temple courts.
67. At age 30, He is baptized in the Jordan River and God's voice comes down from heaven.
68. Jesus begins his public ministry announcing: "The time is fulfilled, and the kingdom of God is at hand: repent ye, and believe the gospel" (Mark 1:14-15 KJV).
69. Jesus teaches about the nature of his kingdom and starts doing its miraculous works.
70. Jesus models how to pray for the kingdom to further come (Matt. 6:9-13).
71. Jesus transfers the kingdom onto others (the twelve and the seventy) and sends them out to proclaim the same kingdom message and do the same works He had been doing.
72. He confers on his first followers a "just as" (same-natured) kingdom (Luke 22:29-30).
73. He instructs them (and us today) using oath language that "he that believeth on me, the works that I do shall he do also; and greater works than these shall he do;" (John 14:12 KJV).
74. He pronounces his Great Commission for his followers, then and there and forever, to "make disciples of all nations" and to "teach them to obey *everything* I have commanded you to do"—please note, it's "everything," not "some things" (Matt. 28:19-20).
75. Then, "at just the right time . . . Christ died" (Rom. 5:6). Everything else that was supposed to happen also happened "at just the right time" as God perfectly foretold—no delays, no gaps, and no exegetical gymnastics need to explain why things expected did not happen.

The Outworking

76. As a result of their kingdom obedience, Jesus' first followers increased into a mighty and world-transforming force.
77. By proclaiming the same gospel message and doing the same works of Jesus and even greater works, along with the supernatural empowerment of the Holy Spirit, they turned the world of their day "upside down . . . . saying that there is another king, *one* Jesus" (Acts 17:6-7 KJV).

78. Then circa A.D. 70, in another dramatic increase of the kingdom coming in power and in precise fulfillment of prophecy, Jesus came "on the clouds" in a day-of-the-Lord, age-ending judgment, and destroyed Jerusalem and the Temple. Thus, the kingdom was taken away from the Jews and "given to a people who will produce its fruit" (Matt. 21:43).

79. The chief priests and the Pharisees "knew he [Jesus] was talking about them" and not to some future generation of Jews (Matt. 21:45b).

80. There is no scriptural promise or prophecy to restore the kingdom to Israel following this removal.

81. The nature of the kingdom, which Jesus presented, was so different from and offensive to what the Jews were expecting, they crucified Him for it. *It is equally different and offensive today.*

82. But was Jesus kidding? Do you really think Jesus expects us Christians today to perform "greater works" than He did, not to mention "the works that I do?" And do you truly think He will hold us accountable for *not* doing these works?

83. We know what his ministry works were. He modeled them for us. Then what are the "greater works?" Speculation abounds. But here's my working definition: The "Greater Works" are—"the works Jesus did *not* do during his earthly ministry, but works God's people have been instructed *to do* throughout Scripture—from the very beginning of the Old Testament to the very end of the New Testament."

84. His "greater works"—in my opinion—can be described in this manner. Those of us who believe in Him are to implement / advance / expand / extend / promote / put into practice his two great eschatological works—that of the kingdom and that of salvation. They encompass the total victory of God through Christ in and over the whole world. Not only are human lives and activities to be transformed, but so is all of society—i.e., lives, laws, institutions, and relationships—social, political, economic, international, etc.

85. In other words, the "greater works" are worldwide societal transformations, or cultural transformations, via advancement of

Christ's everlasting and ever-increasing kingdom and comprehensive salvation.

86. Hence, Jesus did not change the world. What He did was provide the means for his followers to change the world. And his first followers so did.

Following Jesus as He Is Today

87. No longer is Jesus the babe in the manger we celebrate every Christmas, or the boy who played in Galilee, or the man they hung at Calvary, or the lamb who died for you and me. No longer is He the earth-bound, historical Jesus we have come to know and love. Simply put, those views of Jesus are out of date. Make no mistake, that story is important, very important. But that story is also 2,000-year-old history! You see, Jesus is not like that anymore.

88. Nowadays, He is both the same and the greater Jesus. Why is this so? It is because after his virgin birth, earthly life, death, burial, resurrection, and ascension, "God exalted him to the highest place and gave him the name that is above every name that at the name of Jesus every knee should bow, in heaven and on earth, and every tongue confess that Jesus Christ is Lord, to the glory of God the Father" (Phil. 2:8-11; also Eph. 1:20-23). And "so he became as much superior to the angels as the name he has inherited is superior to theirs" (Heb. 1:4).

89. This is Jesus today. He is the ascended, exalted, glorified, transformed, transfigured, transcended, apocalyptic, crowned, and cosmic Christ of the Book of Revelation—the contemporary Christ.

90. We who claim to be followers of Christ today have a high calling to be co-crucified, co-buried, co-resurrected, co-ascended, co-seated with Him in heavenly places in order to be and function as "a kingdom and priests to serve our God, and they will reign on the earth" (Rev. 5:9-10).

91. Anything less is less. But so many Christians have settled for less, to their and our detriment.

92. Going to church is not enough. According to Jesus, the prime purpose and focus of the Christian life is to seek and advance the kingdom of God (Matt. 6:33; John 14:12).
93. However, going to a church can be part of this as long as it enhances this primacy. But going to church and doing church work must not be an end in itself. That reductionist perspective has produced masses of weak, anemic, and lulled-to-sleep pew-sitters, though saved, have not entered the kingdom and consequently have become "less than conquerors."

Turning the World Upside Down, Again

94. In the 1st century, when people observed Christians unified in their proclaiming and living out the reality of the kingdom of God, it was distinctive, drawing, and compelling.
95. This original and unified version of our "once-for-all-delivered faith" (Jude 3) is the model. Its timing and nature must be recovered and reclaimed. Then and only then, might we modern-day Christians be accused of turning the world upside down, again.
96. But flying in the face of everything presented above is the destructive and popular view of cessation theology from both preterist and futurist camps. Its delimitation and devaluation objections and arguments must be emphatically, systematically, and exegetically confronted, refuted, and eradicated.

The Kingdom Pledge of Allegiance

Indeed, the broken places in our world abound and the resulting needs are massive! Consequently, many acknowledge and few doubt that during recent decades America and much of our world have pulled away from their Christian roots and become increasingly secular. But when any nation abandons God and mocks living by his moral standards, moral anarchy and social chaos rear their ugly heads. And so they have. Then what has been the response of many if not most leaders in his Church during this time? One reader of *A Once Mighty Faith* sees it this way: "It really opened my eyes to the missing kingdom teaching as being the main reason why the Church is so impotent." Similarly, my pastor prophetically proclaims, "we are sitting on untapped power!"[6]

This is why I believe the greatest need of the Church universal today is to reclaim the central teaching of Jesus, the kingdom of God—i.e., its full revelation, grounded reality, supernatural power, miraculous gifts, and ministry effectiveness. Indeed, we Christians exist across this planet to repair its broken places. This feat can only be accomplished by advancing Christ's fully established, everlasting, and ever-increasing kingdom. Then we die, go to heaven, and receive our rewards or lack thereof. These "96 New Theses," and the book from which they are largely drawn, are dedicated and directed toward this goal, purpose, and end.

Surely today, the words of Martin Luther, as he stood in defense before the Diet of Worms in 1521, are just as applicable and compelling for the "always reforming" Church:

> *Unless I am convinced by the testimony of the Scriptures or by clear reason (for I do not trust either in the pope or in councils alone, since it is well known that they have often erred and contradicted themselves), I am bound by the Scriptures . . . and my conscience is captive to the Word of God . . . . I cannot do otherwise.*

So will you join us "for such a time as this" and as a pioneering partner as we launch these "96 New Theses for reclaiming Jesus' everlasting kingdom"—this Next Great Reformation? The destiny of America, the world, our children, grandchildren, and future generations, is at stake.

---

[6] Dave Rodriguez, Grace Church, sermon, 10/15-16, 2016.

Here's our kingdom pledge:

> *I pledge allegiance to the kingdom of God*
> *and to the Lord Jesus Christ for which it stands,*
> *one world under God, indivisible in all things,*
> *with liberty and justice, grace and mercy,*
> *love and peace, power and joy for all.*

Once again, I encourage you to read *A Once Mighty Faith* with an open heart and mind. From inside its 437 pages these "96 New Theses" and this pledge are largely drawn. But its expositions on each thesis point will enable you to more fully equip yourself, your leaders, and your congregation to more effectively transform our world for Christ via his fully established, everlasting, and ever-increasing kingdom.

Lastly, of one more thing I am certain—if 21st-century Christians would grasp the significance of Christ's kingdom like 1st-century Christians did, their lives and our world would be utterly transformed.

—Notice to Reader—
You may freely distribute, copy, post, or print the above text:
"96 New Theses for Reclaiming Jesus' Everlasting Kingdom."
Visit PRI's website for downloadable PDF of this booklet at
prophecyrefi.org.

This paperback booklet will also be available as a FREE ebook
for a limited time during the 500th Anniversary year of 2017.

Appendix A

95 Theses from Martin Luther's Great Reformation

Disputation of Doctor Martin Luther
on the Power and Efficacy of Indulgences
by Dr. Martin Luther (1517)
Published in:

Works of Martin Luther:
Adolph Spaeth, L.D. Reed, Henry Eyster Jacobs, et Al., Trans. & Eds.
(Philadelphia: A. J. Holman Company, 1915), Vol.1, pp. 29-38

Out of love for the truth and the desire to bring it to light, the following propositions will be discussed at Wittenberg, under the presidency of the Reverend Father Martin Luther, Master of Arts and of Sacred Theology, and Lecturer in Ordinary on the same at that place. Wherefore he requests that those who are unable to be present and debate orally with us, may do so by letter.

In the Name our Lord Jesus Christ. Amen.

1. Our Lord and Master Jesus Christ, when He said Poenitentiam agite, willed that the whole life of believers should be repentance.

2. This word cannot be understood to mean sacramental penance, i.e., confession and satisfaction, which is administered by the priests.

3. Yet it means not inward repentance only; nay, there is no inward repentance which does not outwardly work divers mortifications of the flesh.

4. The penalty [of sin], therefore, continues so long as hatred of self continues; for this is the true inward repentance, and continues until our entrance into the kingdom of heaven.

5. The pope does not intend to remit, and cannot remit any penalties other than those which he has imposed either by his own authority or by that of the Canons.

6. The pope cannot remit any guilt, except by declaring that it has been remitted by God and by assenting to God's remission; though, to be sure, he may grant remission in cases reserved to his judgment. If his right to grant remission in such cases were despised, the guilt would remain entirely unforgiven.

7. God remits guilt to no one whom He does not, at the same time, humble in all things and bring into subjection to His vicar, the priest.

8. The penitential canons are imposed only on the living, and, according to them, nothing should be imposed on the dying.

9. Therefore the Holy Spirit in the pope is kind to us, because in his decrees he always makes exception of the article of death and of necessity.

10. Ignorant and wicked are the doings of those priests who, in the case of the dying, reserve canonical penances for purgatory.

11. This changing of the canonical penalty to the penalty of purgatory is quite evidently one of the tares that were sown while the bishops slept.

12. In former times the canonical penalties were imposed not after, but before absolution, as tests of true contrition.

13. The dying are freed by death from all penalties; they are already dead to canonical rules, and have a right to be released from them.

14. The imperfect health [of soul], that is to say, the imperfect love, of the dying brings with it, of necessity, great fear; and the smaller the love, the greater is the fear.

15. This fear and horror is sufficient of itself alone (to say nothing of other things) to constitute the penalty of purgatory, since it is very near to the horror of despair.

16. Hell, purgatory, and heaven seem to differ as do despair, almost-despair, and the assurance of safety.

17. With souls in purgatory it seems necessary that horror should grow less and love increase.

18. It seems unproved, either by reason or Scripture, that they are outside the state of merit, that is to say, of increasing love.

19. Again, it seems unproved that they, or at least that all of them, are certain or assured of their own blessedness, though we may be quite certain of it.

20. Therefore by "full remission of all penalties" the pope means not actually "of all," but only of those imposed by himself.

21. Therefore those preachers of indulgences are in error, who say that by the pope's indulgences a man is freed from every penalty, and saved;

22. Whereas he remits to souls in purgatory no penalty which, according to the canons, they would have had to pay in this life.

23. If it is at all possible to grant to any one the remission of all penalties whatsoever, it is certain that this remission can be granted only to the most perfect, that is, to the very fewest.

24. It must needs be, therefore, that the greater part of the people are deceived by that indiscriminate and highsounding promise of release from penalty.

25. The power which the pope has, in a general way, over purgatory, is just like the power which any bishop or curate has, in a special way, within his own diocese or parish.

26. The pope does well when he grants remission to souls [in purgatory], not by the power of the keys (which he does not possess), but by way of intercession.

27. They preach man who say that so soon as the penny jingles into the money-box, the soul flies out [of purgatory].

28. It is certain that when the penny jingles into the money-box, gain and avarice can be increased, but the result of the intercession of the Church is in the power of God alone.

29. Who knows whether all the souls in purgatory wish to be bought out of it, as in the legend of Sts. Severinus and Paschal.

30. No one is sure that his own contrition is sincere; much less that he has attained full remission.

31. Rare as is the man that is truly penitent, so rare is also the man who truly buys indulgences, i.e., such men are most rare.

32. They will be condemned eternally, together with their teachers, who believe themselves sure of their salvation because they have letters of pardon.

33. Men must be on their guard against those who say that the pope's pardons are that inestimable gift of God by which man is reconciled to Him;

34. For these "graces of pardon" concern only the penalties of sacramental satisfaction, and these are appointed by man.

35. They preach no Christian doctrine who teach that contrition is not necessary in those who intend to buy souls out of purgatory or to buy confessionalia.

36. Every truly repentant Christian has a right to full remission of penalty and guilt, even without letters of pardon.

37. Every true Christian, whether living or dead, has part in all the blessings of Christ and the Church; and this is granted him by God, even without letters of pardon.

38. Nevertheless, the remission and participation [in the blessings of the Church] which are granted by the pope are in no way to be despised, for they are, as I have said, the declaration of divine remission.

39. It is most difficult, even for the very keenest theologians, at one and the same time to commend to the people the abundance of pardons and [the need of] true contrition.

40. True contrition seeks and loves penalties, but liberal pardons only relax penalties and cause them to be hated, or at least, furnish an occasion [for hating them].

41. Apostolic pardons are to be preached with caution, lest the people may falsely think them preferable to other good works of love.

42. Christians are to be taught that the pope does not intend the buying of pardons to be compared in any way to works of mercy.

43. Christians are to be taught that he who gives to the poor or lends to the needy does a better work than buying pardons;

44. Because love grows by works of love, and man becomes better; but by pardons man does not grow better, only more free from penalty.

45. Christians are to be taught that he who sees a man in need, and passes him by, and gives [his money] for pardons, purchases not the indulgences of the pope, but the indignation of God.

46. Christians are to be taught that unless they have more than they need, they are bound to keep back what is necessary for their own families, and by no means to squander it on pardons.
47. Christians are to be taught that the buying of pardons is a matter of free will, and not of commandment.
48. Christians are to be taught that the pope, in granting pardons, needs, and therefore desires, their devout prayer for him more than the money they bring.
49. Christians are to be taught that the pope's pardons are useful, if they do not put their trust in them: but altogether harmful, if through them they lose their fear of God.
50. Christians are to be taught that if the pope knew the exactions of the pardon-preachers, he would rather that St. Peter's church should go to ashes, than that it should be built up with the skin, flesh and bones of his sheep.
51. Christians are to be taught that it would be the pope's wish, as it is his duty, to give of his own money to very many of those from whom certain hawkers of pardons cajole money, even though the church of St. Peter might have to be sold.
52. The assurance of salvation by letters of pardon is vain, even though the commissary, nay, even though the pope himself, were to stake his soul upon it.
53. They are enemies of Christ and of the pope, who bid the Word of God be altogether silent in some Churches, in order that pardons may be preached in others.
54. Injury is done the Word of God when, in the same sermon, an equal or a longer time is spent on pardons than on this Word.
55. It must be the intention of the pope that if pardons, which are a very small thing, are celebrated with one bell, with single processions and ceremonies, then the Gospel, which is the very greatest thing, should be preached with a hundred bells, a hundred processions, a hundred ceremonies.
56. The "treasures of the Church," out of which the pope grants indulgences, are not sufficiently named or known among the people of Christ.
57. That they are not temporal treasures is certainly evident, for many of the vendors do not pour out such treasures so easily, but only gather them.

58. Nor are they the merits of Christ and the Saints, for even without the pope, these always work grace for the inner man, and the cross, death, and hell for the outward man.
59. St. Lawrence said that the treasures of the Church were the Church's poor, but he spoke according to the usage of the word in his own time.
60. Without rashness we say that the keys of the Church, given by Christ's merit, are that treasure;
61. For it is clear that for the remission of penalties and of reserved cases, the power of the pope is of itself sufficient.
62. The true treasure of the Church is the Most Holy Gospel of the glory and the grace of God.
63. But this treasure is naturally most odious, for it makes the first to be last.
64. On the other hand, the treasure of indulgences is naturally most acceptable, for it makes the last to be first.
65. Therefore the treasures of the Gospel are nets with which they formerly were wont to fish for men of riches.
66. The treasures of the indulgences are nets with which they now fish for the riches of men.
67. The indulgences which the preachers cry as the "greatest graces" are known to be truly such, in so far as they promote gain.
68. Yet they are in truth the very smallest graces compared with the grace of God and the piety of the Cross.
69. Bishops and curates are bound to admit the commissaries of apostolic pardons, with all reverence.
70. But still more are they bound to strain all their eyes and attend with all their ears, lest these men preach their own dreams instead of the commission of the pope.
71. He who speaks against the truth of apostolic pardons, let him be anathema and accursed!
72. But he who guards against the lust and license of the pardon-preachers, let him be blessed!
73. The pope justly thunders against those who, by any art, contrive the injury of the traffic in pardons.
74. But much more does he intend to thunder against those who use the pretext of pardons to contrive the injury of holy love and truth.

75. To think the papal pardons so great that they could absolve a man even if he had committed an impossible sin and violated the Mother of God -- this is madness.

76. We say, on the contrary, that the papal pardons are not able to remove the very least of venial sins, so far as its guilt is concerned.

77. It is said that even St. Peter, if he were now Pope, could not bestow greater graces; this is blasphemy against St. Peter and against the pope.

78. We say, on the contrary, that even the present pope, and any pope at all, has greater graces at his disposal; to wit, the Gospel, powers, gifts of healing, etc., as it is written in I. Corinthians xii.

79. To say that the cross, emblazoned with the papal arms, which is set up [by the preachers of indulgences], is of equal worth with the Cross of Christ, is blasphemy.

80. The bishops, curates and theologians who allow such talk to be spread among the people, will have an account to render.

81. This unbridled preaching of pardons makes it no easy matter, even for learned men, to rescue the reverence due to the pope from slander, or even from the shrewd questionings of the laity.

82. To wit: -- "Why does not the pope empty purgatory, for the sake of holy love and of the dire need of the souls that are there, if he redeems an infinite number of souls for the sake of miserable money with which to build a Church? The former reasons would be most just; the latter is most trivial."

83. Again: -- "Why are mortuary and anniversary masses for the dead continued, and why does he not return or permit the withdrawal of the endowments founded on their behalf, since it is wrong to pray for the redeemed?"

84. Again: -- "What is this new piety of God and the pope, that for money they allow a man who is impious and their enemy to buy out of purgatory the pious soul of a friend of God, and do not rather, because of that pious and beloved soul's own need, free it for pure love's sake?"

85. Again: -- "Why are the penitential canons long since in actual fact and through disuse abrogated and dead, now satisfied by the granting of indulgences, as though they were still alive and in force?"

86. Again: -- "Why does not the pope, whose wealth is to-day greater than the riches of the richest, build just this one church of St. Peter with his own money, rather than with the money of poor believers?"

87. Again: -- "What is it that the pope remits, and what participation does he grant to those who, by perfect contrition, have a right to full remission and participation?"

88. Again: -- "What greater blessing could come to the Church than if the pope were to do a hundred times a day what he now does once, and bestow on every believer these remissions and participations?"

89. "Since the pope, by his pardons, seeks the salvation of souls rather than money, why does he suspend the indulgences and pardons granted heretofore, since these have equal efficacy?"

90. To repress these arguments and scruples of the laity by force alone, and not to resolve them by giving reasons, is to expose the Church and the pope to the ridicule of their enemies, and to make Christians unhappy.

91. If, therefore, pardons were preached according to the spirit and mind of the pope, all these doubts would be readily resolved; nay, they would not exist.

92. Away, then, with all those prophets who say to the people of Christ, "Peace, peace," and there is no peace!

93. Blessed be all those prophets who say to the people of Christ, "Cross, cross," and there is no cross!

94. Christians are to be exhorted that they be diligent in following Christ, their Head, through penalties, deaths, and hell;

95. And thus be confident of entering into heaven rather through many tribulations, than through the assurance of peace.

PROJECT WITTENBERG

Appendix B

'Mighty Revival Coming Your Way'

Eleven years ago, the publisher of my first book, *Peak Performance Principles for High Achievers* (1984) asked me to write an expanded edition. He proposed that I report back to my over 180,000 readers (at that time) on how those "fabulous" principles have worked out in my life during that intervening 21-year period. This expanded second edition, based on that premise, was published in 2006.

I cannot think of a better way to wrap up this booklet, *The Next Great Reformation*, than by sharing with you an excerpt from that edition. It's about a night that ranks as one of my most unforgettable. That night literally changed the trajectory of my life. My hope is this excerpt from a chapter I added back then will shed light on what I consider to be my major motivation and constantly prayed-for anointing for writing books and creating a body of knowledge (see pp. 45-46). My pastor, Dave Rodriguez (see p. 8), terms this growing body of knowledge my "destiny and legacy." Also please know one other thing. I write as a committed follower of Jesus Christ—my Savior, Lord, and King.

Beginning of Excerpt

When I originally contemplated writing this second edition, I never intended to go public with this next personal story. Some people may be troubled by it. But I feel compelled to include it. You see, it laid the foundation for the redirection of my life during the past 21 years.

"MIGHTY REVIVAL COMING YOUR WAY" the sign announced. "Prophetic Teaching, Words of Knowledge and Discerning of Spirits," the newspaper advertisement proclaimed. "Bring the Sick; Witness With Your Own Eyes – The Miracle Power of the Healing Christ."

I'd never seen or heard anything like this in my church. Could it be genuine? Or was it a fraud? I had to find out for myself.

"Don't go," my conservative Christian friends warned me. "You'll just contaminate your ministry."

In retrospect, they were right. Somehow they knew that if I went, I'd no longer be able to settle for the common, the ordinary, the dull, or the spectator role in the area of my faith. Maybe it was my well-preserved sense of childlike wonder and adventurous spirit that explained my intense desire to know, and to know for sure. I had to stop accepting other people's opinions about something this important. I had to go and see for myself. So on a Friday night in the mid-1980s, full of doubts and a little nervous about the whole thing, my wife and I drove to the "Mighty Revival."

The room was only half full. We entered from the back and sat about half way down next to the center aisle. I reckon 75 to 100 people were in attendance. Please understand something very important. We didn't know a soul and they didn't know us, either.

The meeting was totally different from anything we'd ever witnessed—people jumping, shouting, singing, dancing, waving their hands. People in our church didn't act that way. After the sermon and toward the end of the service the preacher asked everyone to close their eyes and bow their heads. Then he began to walk around the meeting room, all the time ministering in a booming voice to various people. He told them personal, intimate details about their lives and about people in their families. I figured he probably knew them. But he didn't know us.

A short time later, I could hear his voice coming up the center aisle. He was talking about the Apostle John in the Bible and walked right past me. Then, he stopped, turned around, walked back, and stood beside me. My eyes were still closed and my head still bowed. The next thing I knew, he grabbed my left hand and raised it straight up into the air. All the while he kept talking about the Apostle John, and in a loud voice that everyone could hear.

Suddenly, he stopped speaking to the group, squeezed my hand and addressed me personally, "JOHN! JOHN! JOHN, GOD HAS GIVEN

YOU SPECIAL REVELATION OF SCRIPTURE. YOU ARE TO TEACH TO OTHERS, TO A LOT OF PEOPLE AND TO YOUR FAMILY, JOHN."

I sat frozen in my seat, eyes still dutifully closed, head bowed, my hand held high in the air by his. Next, almost without missing a breath, he started talking about Noah, "GOD HAD ANOTHER GREAT SON, NOAH," he roared.

My mind flashed back to the first time my father told my little brother and I that our family name was in the Bible. We figured he was kidding. But he wasn't. He showed us in the King James Version of the New Testament, where Noah's name is written as "Noe" (see Matthew 24:37, 38, for example).

Again, he squeezed my hand and in a loud voice declared, "JOHN NOAH! RECEIVE THIS ANOINTING!" I still couldn't believe what I was hearing. He put the two names of the two biblical characters he had been talking about together, and it was my name. Wow! Could this be, I thought. It was certainly more than a coincidence.

"STOP RESISTING IT," he admonished me while squeezing my hand even harder, "RECEIVE THIS ANOINTING."

Then it was over. He let go of my hand, walked back up the aisle toward the front, and began speaking to someone else. Please understand, once again, I didn't know him and he didn't know me. Furthermore, no one in that room knew me or my wife. I don't know how you would have felt, but I didn't know what to think. I was in somewhat of a daze. Slowly, I leaned over to my wife and whispered, "Do you know who he was talking to? He was talking to me. He was holding my hand up in the air."

"Yes, I know," she replied.

"I peeked," she admitted.

If that wasn't enough, about 10 minutes later the preacher leaned over the top of his pulpit, pointed down over the top of the rows straight at my wife, and called her by name too. Then he bellowed out for all to hear, "CINDY, THE FIRE OF GOD IS GOING UP AND DOWN YOUR BACK. YOU ARE BEING HEALED THIS VERY MOMENT, AND YOU ARE TO TEACH TOO."

Needless to say, our drive home that night was anything but normal. "I could hardly breathe when he was talking to me," she related. "It felt like a giant weight was on my chest the whole time."

Whatever actually happened that night to my wife and me at the "Mighty Revival," one thing is sure; it was an event that was so remarkable, so unbelievable, and yet so real that we could not dismiss it. Years later, I am better able to understand that this experience was my first dramatic encounter with what many consider to be the supernatural. That night my wife and I had tasted a reality that is denied or ignored by most of our Bible-belt friends and close advisers. But, at the time, I wondered, *Was this of God? Or was it a fraud, occultic, or spiritism?* Now I'm convinced it was from God. Surprisingly and with a bang, I had tapped into a new, different, and exciting dimension! It forever changed the way I thought of myself, understood God's Word, the Bible, and saw the world around me.

Yes, it was like donning another new set of eyeglasses through which I began to re-examine all I'd been taught. Supernaturally, the Spirit of wisdom and revelation began to flow through me as never before (Eph. 1:17). The eyes of my heart grew more and more enlightened (Eph. 1:18). Ever since this experience at the "Mighty Revival," I have often found myself contemplating, *What was it that God has called "John Noah (Noe) to teach to others, to a lot of people and to your family?"*

My Quest for Truth and Understanding

After I became a Christian, for sure, back in the 1980s, a lot of what I was hearing was: "Time is short. We don't have much time left."

"How do you know?" I asked.

"Because we are living in the 'last days!'" I was told. "These are the end times. Jesus is coming back and taking us out of here. Soon it will be over. We are leaving this world."

It was the heyday of Hal Lindsey's book, *The Late Great Planet Earth*. And this end-times-gospel was everywhere, at least everywhere in the circles in which I was traveling. I remember thinking at the time, *Oh, no!* I had just become a Christian. The business my wife and I started five years ago was now making money. Our two children were in grade school. I wanted to see them grow up. I didn't want everything to end, not yet.

Then my daughter transferred to a Christian school. She began hearing so much of this termination message that for several years she was convinced she would never have to make plans to go to college and would never get married. Today, she is happily married, has three children, and has earned a master's degree.

Back then I was also being taught to read and study my Bible. That is when a strange thing started to happen. Contrary verses began popping out to me like this one from Hebrews 1:1-2: "In the past God spoke to our forefathers through the prophets at many times and in various ways, but in these last days he has spoken to us by his Son."

So I started asking questions to those I deemed were in the know.

"Doesn't the writer of Hebrews state here that the biblical time frame known as the 'last days' was taking place, back then and there— i.e. during the earthly ministry of Jesus and during the time he was writing? And if that is true, how can we possibly say we are now living in the 'last days?'"

"Well, we just are! Look around," I was bluntly advised. "It doesn't take a genius to figure this out. Just look at the moral decay in society today or world events. How could you come up with any other conclusion? Everybody knows we are living in the 'last days.'"

But I found this response very unsatisfying. The answer of another Christian leader, however, seemed to make more sense. He assured me that the "last days" were present in the 1st Century. But they stopped.

"When and how?" I queried.

"When the Jews rejected the kingdom Jesus was bringing and crucified Him, God's prophetic time clock stopped ticking and everything—the kingdom and 'these last days'—was postponed and put on hold," he replied with confidence. "But the 'last days' started up again."

"When?" I asked, again.

"In 1948, when Israel was re-birthed as a nation. And soon, Jesus will return and set up his kingdom here on earth, in Jerusalem," he further explained.

His explanation seemed plausible until I got home. That is when it hit me. The writer of Hebrews was writing some 30 to 35 years after Jesus' crucifixion and after this claimed postponement event. I also soon discovered that other inspired Scripture, again written some 20 to 30 years after that time, was still presenting the kingdom as a then-present and viable reality. For example, the Apostle Paul after his three missionary journeys was still "boldly and without hindrance" preaching "the kingdom of God" and teaching "about the Lord Jesus Christ" (Acts

28:31). Apparently, if what I was being told was correct, somebody, like Peter or the Holy Spirit, forgot to clue in Paul that the kingdom had been postponed (also see Acts 1:3; 19:8; Heb. 12:28.) Besides, I pondered, how are Christians today supposed to follow Jesus' admonition to "seek first his kingdom and his righteousness" (Matt. 6:33) if this kingdom is still in a postponed status?

A few months later, I discovered another view. "Sure, they were living in the 'last days' back then," one pastor agreed. "And we have been living in them ever since."

Needless to say, the more questions I raised about "these last days" and other related end-time topics, the more I began to sense that many of my Christian friends did not appreciate my inquisitiveness.

"If you keep this up," one warned me, "you'll only get more confused and confuse many others."

I admit this admonishment was intimidating. *Maybe I'm being too critical*, I agonized. After all, I was a new Christian. What did I know? And everyone I knew believed this end-time-gospel message. All the popular Christian books proclaimed it. The TV preachers preached it. We *must* be living in the "last days." It seemed so logical. But I also knew that the answers I was getting simply did not match up to what the Bible actually said.

So over the past 20 or so years I have been on a somewhat relentless quest for truth and understanding in the theological area known as eschatology (the study of last things). My pursuit has led me around the country and across the paths of many people. During this time, I have asked many more tough questions, written a few books, delivered 20 theological papers, and spoken at numerous conferences—all on issues of eschatological reform.

Confirmation and Criticism

During this time, I've invested countless hours in hard study, intensive research, and serious inquiry [and prayer]. I've fought my way through piles of conflicting views and contrasting opinions, all from learned writers. And I have sought out expert guides, intellectual leaders, and respected theologians, many of whom I have worked with quite closely. Below is a sample of comments, positive and negative, that some have written concerning either my book titled *The Apocalypse*

Conspiracy (1991) or my book titled *Beyond the End Times: The Rest of . . . the Greatest Story Ever Told* (1999):

Positive Confirmations

"Noe's book just could be the spark that ignites the next reformation of Christianity."

> – James Earl Massey, former Sr. Editor *Christianity Today* Dean Emeritus, School of Theology, Anderson University & Distinguished Professor-at-Large

"Your treatment of the 'end of the world' is the best treatment of this idea that I had read that I can remember. Your book could really open the eyes of a lot of people."

> – Walter C. Hibbard, former Chairman, Great Christian Books

"If people in the churches can be persuaded to take another look at the relationship between our present experience and our future hope, I think they will see that your perspective is far more on target than they may at first realize. In order to see this, however, they will have to be willing to have questions raised about the assumptions which have simply been repeated but not examined by the last few generations of evangelicals."

> – Arden C. Autry, former Associate Professor of Biblical Literature, Oral Roberts University

"This is an important work . . . You make an impressive case for your major point. That point is being made practically nowhere else in evangelical Christianity (to my knowledge) and it deserves to be made and discussed."

> – Ron Allen, Associate Professor Preaching and New Testament Christian Theological Seminary

. . . .

Negative Criticisms

Some of these are quite severe. But over the years, I've learned that critics should not just humble us, but sharpen us. I've also learned how to listen to them and to hear through what they are saying. I will quote a few, anonymously, however:

"A tremendous tragedy will occur if Noe's theory gains widespread acceptance."

"I believe your book will be used as a tool of Satan to teach concepts that are in direct violation of God's word."

"You take an approach which is diametrically opposed to _____ Ministries."

"I feel like I've had my favorite easy chair pulled out from underneath me."

"Noe's book raises more problems than it solves. It promotes a position which, according to all the historic Christian creeds—Protestant, Catholic, or Orthodox—is heterodox."

"I do not see your book contributing significantly to the dialogue. It's too confrontational to really help make progress."

"He presents nothing new, but he does package it cleverly. These ideas have been floating around for centuries. All he's done is conflate them . . . It won't fly." . . . .

"You are not ready for the intensity of debate this book will precipitate. It is going to make matters worse. . . ."

" . . . what you're saying devastates my theology . . . but you are more literal than we are." . . . .

Such is the nature of high achievement in any field of endeavor—business, politics, education, or even in theology. Criticism and intimidation are part of the deal. Those who will not step outside customary boundaries will be upset and will ostracize anyone who does. Being one of the principal advocates for the next reformation of Christianity, as Dr. Massey alluded to above, is no exception. But how's that for a God-sized goal?

Sad to say, in the field of theology, the tendency to demonize others with whom you disagree is far too common. Much of it stems from professional jealousy and tradition-bound defensiveness. It is so easy to merely continue mouthing our particular tradition rather than to endure the hard work and pain of reassessment, critical thinking, and sincerely praying for and following "the Spirit of wisdom and revelation" (Eph. 1:17). The 18th Century French philosopher, Voltaire, hit it on the head when he surmised:

> Our wretched species is so made that those who walk on the well-trodden path always throw stones at those who are showing a new road.

In other words, if you dare confront conventional beliefs, some, perhaps many, will oppose you, react against you, and even attack you personally. That's to be expected. And that's not all bad. What's important is that you respond in love, with sincerity, and in a measured tone. But I believe God has provided me with profound insights on topics of utmost importance. Accordingly, I intend to step out in the gifting He has bestowed.

Furthermore, I don't believe it is wrong to question long-held beliefs and challenge traditions. After all, the Bible tells us to "test everything. Hold on to the good . . ." (1 Thess. 5:21). Nothing should be exempt. If something we've accepted through tradition cannot be defended, it's a good sign we need to reconsider it. Truth must not be based upon blind acceptance but upon solid evidence. If something is really true, it will stand up under testing.

Cautiously, however, I'm reminded of the admonishment the Italian statesman, Machiavelli, wrote in his famous 16th-century book, *The Prince*, chapter six:

There is nothing more difficult to take in hand, more perilous to conduct, or more uncertain in its success, than to take the lead in the introduction of a new order of things.

It is for a "new order of things"—the next reformation of Christianity—that I am "one crying in the cornfields," similar to John the Baptist in his day who was characterized as "one crying in the wilderness" (Matt. 3:3). Then there was Martin Luther, who in his day cried out for reform in the Church.

Make no mistake, however, I am not equating myself with them. But I do identify with them and other great pioneers. In their days, many thought that John the Baptist and Martin Luther were crazy or worse. Many today think that of me. But this new mountain of reformation is quite an undertaking. It is one I cannot climb alone. Most likely, I won't reach the summit, at least in my lifetime. John the Baptist didn't. Martin Luther didn't, either. Great ideas and God-sized goals take time. But climb, I will. Help prepare the way for others who will follow, I will also. But I won't give up. I must endure to the end, so help me God![1]

End of Excerpt

Is This God's Perfect and Appointed Time?

During the past 30 years what happened that night at the "Mighty Revival" remains my major motivation and constantly prayed-for anointing for writing books—especially the one from which the "96 New Theses" are largely drawn. All together, these books form a body of knowledge. I hope and pray these published books will someday contribute to the reclamation of Jesus' everlasting kingdom and reestablishment of our "a once mighty faith."

In this regard, here is one of my favorite quotes. I cited it in *A Once Mighty Faith*. In a nutshell and in 1997, I believe Tony Evans best captured America's current situation thusly:

---

[1] John Noē, *Peak Performance Principles for High Achievers – Revised Edition* (Hollywood, FL.: Frederick Fell Publishers, Inc., 2006), 166-178.

Let me put the problem to you in the form of a question. How can we have all these churches on all these street corners, filled with all these members, led by all these preachers, elders, and deacons . . . and yet still have all this mess in America? Something is wrong somewhere!

But when we turn the education of our children over to the state, and the state removes biblical ethics from its curriculum, what you get is the mess we have now. . . . This is what is happening in America today. The glory of the Lord is on its way out.[2]

In 2016, the Reverend Billy Graham concurred. In his syndicated newspaper column he cautiously and tactfully warned:

Yes, in recent decades our nation certainly has been drifting from its Judeo-Christian roots, and in many ways has become increasingly secular. We've come to tolerate attitudes and ways of living that would have been frowned upon only a few generations ago. . . .

And eventually we will pay a price for this, because when a nation abandons God, it also abandons living by God's moral standards. And once this happens, we could end up in moral anarchy and social chaos.[3]

Additionally in 2016, the Billy Graham Evangelistic Association ratcheted up the severity of our country's situation with its "Decision America Tour 2016 with Franklin Graham." This tour held prayer rallies in all 50 state capitals to "wake up America," "to share the gospel and challenge Christians to pray fervently and boldly live out their faith," and to encourage Christians to "vote" and "engage." Why so? Because, as their tour packet explained, "our nation is in trouble, and the answer doesn't rest in our politicians and political parties."

During his comments at the October 5th rally held here in Indianapolis on the lawn and steps of our State Capitol Building, Dr. Graham decried: "America is being stripped of its godly heritage. . . . We've turned our back on God. . . . [and] God doesn't need compromising Christians."

Indeed, as far back as 1999 (see Dedication, p. iii), others and I were contemplating and talking about the great need for this Next Great Reformation. But now in 2017 the time for its reclamation and launching

---

[2] Tony Evans, *What a Way to Live!* (Nashville, TN.: Word Publishing, 1997), 294, 76, 251.

[3] Billy Graham, "My Answer," *The Indianapolis Star*, 10/15/16, 4E.

may be God's perfect and appointed time. Therefore, will you join with us in helping get the word out about and be part of this potentially significant, historical movement and moment—"for such a time as this"—as we boldly step up, step out, and attempt to reclaim Jesus' everlasting kingdom and our "a once mighty faith." God willing!

If so, I'd love to hear from you.

CONTACT US:

Prophecy Reformation Institute
5236 East 72nd Street
Indianapolis, IN 46250
Website: prophecyrefi.org
jnoe@prophecyrefi.org
Ph. # 317-842-3411

—Notice to Reader—
This paperback booklet will also be available as a FREE ebook on Amazon.com and downloadable PDF on PRI's website for a limited time during the 500th Anniversary year of 2017.

A Body of Knowledge from John Noē

*The Next Great Reformation: *96 New Theses for reclaiming Jesus' everlasting kingdom*

*A Once Mighty Faith: *Reclaiming the central teaching of Jesus, reengaging the miraculous*

*The Creation of Evil: *Casting light into the purposes of darkness*

Unraveling the End: *A balanced scholarly synthesis of four competing and conflicting end-time views*

*The Greater Jesus: *His glorious unveiling*

Off Target: *18 bull's-eye exposés*

*Hell Yes / Hell No: *What really is the extent of God's grace . . . and wrath?*

The Perfect Ending for the World

Peak Performance Principles for High Achievers – Revised Edition (2006)

Available on Amazon.com

*In paperback and ebook.

See the reviews, "Look Inside," and read more about each book.

Also check out PRI's website at: prophecyrefi.org.

What's Upcoming?

Into the Great Beyond: Unlocking life's last great adventure

Transcending the Limits of Self: Becoming all you were created to be

The Israel Illusion: Pulling back the curtain on the land of God

The Scene Behind the Seen: A Preterist-Idealist commentary of the Book of Revelation—unveiling its fulfillment and ongoing relevance— past, present & future

'TRAITOR WARRIOR'
The Days of Vengeance—The back story, theology, and script behind the proposed movie

???

Books Out-of-Print

Beyond the End Times
    (re-titled, revised, expanded – *The Perfect Ending for the World*)
The Apocalypse Conspiracy
    (re-titled, revised, expanded – *The Greater Jesus*)
Shattering the 'Left Behind' Delusion
Dead in Their Tracks
People Power
Peak Performance Principles for High Achievers
    (1986, 1984 original mass market and hardcover editions)